Pop-up Cards
& Invitations

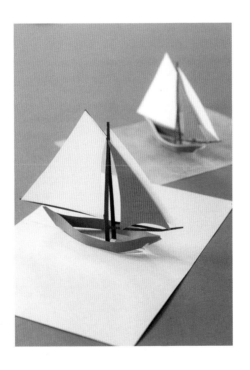

Maurice Mathon

STACKPOLE
BOOKS

Published by
STACKPOLE BOOKS
5067 Ritter Road
Mechanicsburg, PA 17055
www.stackpolebooks.com

Printed in G. Canale & C, EU.

10 9 8 7 6 5 4 3 2 1

First edition

Dessain et Tolra/Larousse
Edited by: Corinne de Montalembert, assisted by Johana Sellem
Proofreading: Madeleine Biaujeaud
Pagination: Bénédicte Chantalou/Yuruga
Photography: Fabrice Besse
Design: Sonia Roy
Cover design: Véronique Laporte
Fabrication: Anne Raynaud

Stackpole Books
Translation: Kathryn Fulton
Pagination and cover design: Tessa Sweigert

Cataloging-in-Publication Data is on file with the Library of Congress

ISBN 978-0-8117-1071-8

Introduction

Cards that are fun to make, to send, to receive, and to keep. Cards to look at, to put on a shelf, a dresser, a mantlepiece. Cards that surprise and delight every time you open them.

Originating in China and Japan, cutting and folding paper are traditional techniques, probably as old as paper itself. Combining cutting and folding, the pop-up card appeared first in England in the nineteenth century, in the lively pictures in children's books, then in the twentieth century in greeting cards and announcements. At the end of the twentieth century, some artists, notably Japanese ones, renewed the form and raised the pop-up to a full-fledged art.

In this book, you will find the patterns for 20 original creations and 15 detachable pre-printed cards that require no gluing or assembly.

Contents

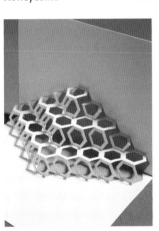

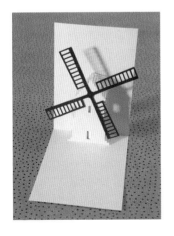

For each project, the
level of difficulty is
shown:

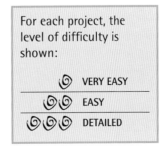	VERY EASY
	EASY
	DETAILED

How to fold the detachable pop-up cards

1. You will need a craft knife or utility knife, a cutting board, a standard ruler, a fine embossing stylus (available at craft centers), and a small metal ruler.

2. Detach the chosen page and place it on the cutting board.

3. Use the craft knife to cut along the solid lines.

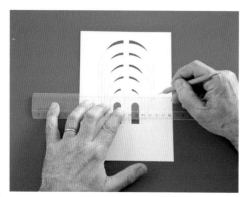

4. Use the stylus to score along the dotted lines.

FOLDS

Always make the folds in the right direction:
- valley = \/ (---)
- mountain = /\ (...)

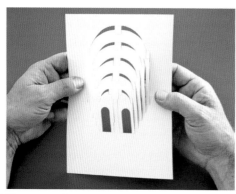

5. Use your fingers to check that all the cut lines come apart easily, and go over them again with the craft knife if necessary.

6. Using the small ruler or gently pinching the paper between your fingers, make the folds a little at a time, paying close attention to which kind of fold it is: "valley" (---) or "mountain" (...). Be careful not to fold the paper outside of these lines.

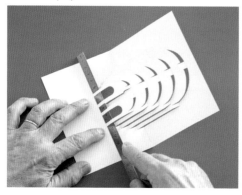

7. When the card stands up, with the two sides forming a 90-degree angle, continue to fold each fold a little bit at a time until the card is folded up on itself completely.

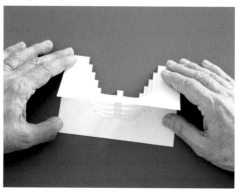

8. Turn the card 180 degrees, with the opening facing toward you, then open the card.

After you close it up again the card can be slid into an ordinary envelope.

Pyramid

Ampitheater

Cathedral Doors

White Flowers

Forest

Beach House

Waterwheel

European Houses

Angels

Russian Church

Baby's Room

Castle

Mushrooms

Japanese Garden

Lighthouse

General Techniques

Tools and Materials

1. Cutting board
2. Small metal ruler
3. Ordinary craft knife
4. Precision craft knife
5. Pencil
6. Standard ruler
7. Fine-tipped embossing stylus
8. Glue stick
9. Tape
10. Sewing thread
11. Fine needle
12. Scissors
13. Tweezers
14. Paper clips

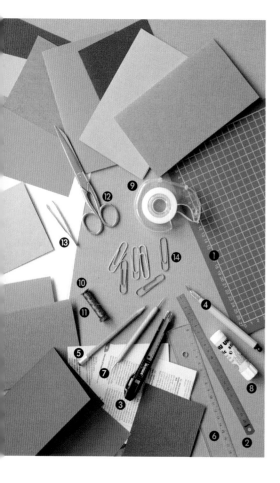

Papers

For the decorations, any kind of paper can be used. For the card itself, you can use paper from 120g to 210g, but the ideal weight is 160g. Make sure you have some scrap paper on hand as well.

Cutting

Attach the pattern on top of the paper that you're going to cut. This method lets you avoid having to transfer the pattern onto the paper and then erase it later. Use a scanner or photocopier to reproduce the chosen pattern at the necessary scale on 80g white paper.

Hold the pattern in place with large paper clips that won't leave marks on the paper, or with small pieces of repositionable adhesive. For cutting, you will need a cutting board and a ruler.

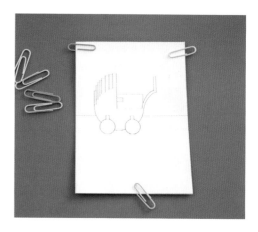

The cuts need to be clean and precise. An ordinary craft knife will work well, in general, especially for straight lines and wide curves.

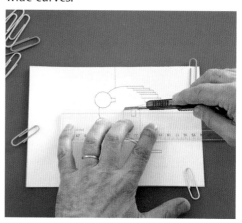

For the details, a precision craft knife with a small, pointed blade, possibly pivoting, is indispensable.

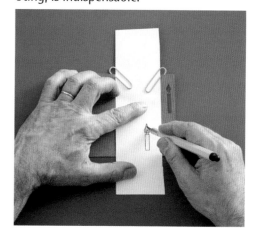

Scoring

Marking the folds is a very important step. Use a ruler and a fine-tipped embossing stylus.

First score the project with the pattern still attched to the paper, after cutting it. This will allow you to mark the placement of the folds with precision.

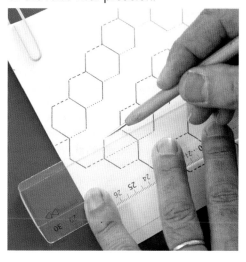

Score again, after taking the pattern off, to mark the folds well. Push hard—paper is generally very resistant to scraping. Even if this seems long and fastidious, these two scoring steps are absolutely indispendable. A good scoring job makes the folding much easier. Inversely, it is practically impossible to fold a badly scored card.

Folding

The cards in this book are of two types:
• Opening at 180 degrees: the open card is flat, the two halves forming an 180-degree angle.

• Opening at 90 degrees: the two halves of the card form an angle of 90 degrees; the principal fold of the card can be horizontal or vertical.

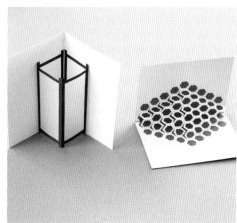

To fold the card, use your fingers, the small ruler, or, occasionally, the tweezers.

For 90-degree cards, make each fold progressively. It is very important to pay attention to the direction of the folds as they appear on the pattern or detachable card—"valley" folds (---) and "mountain" folds (...)—and to make sure to not bend the paper outside of the indicated folds.

Don't try to bend each fold back on itself completely before moving on to the next one. You need to gently fold all the folds, one after another, and then come back to the first folds to accentuate each fold a bit; go back through all the folds again and again until the card is folded completely over on itself. Crease the folds well by pressing down on them, then open the card to 90 degrees.

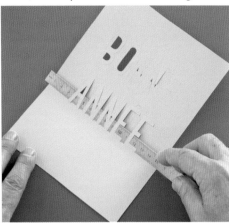

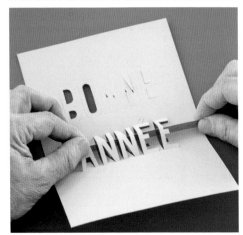

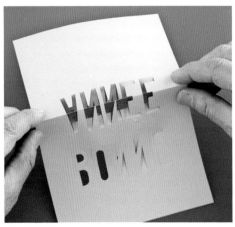

Gluing

When gluing with the glue stick, use a piece of scrap paper or a page of an old magazine underneath so that you can go over the edges of the piece. Throw this sheet away after each use. You can cover up the parts of the piece that should not be glued with another piece of scrap paper.

To fix a partial glue job, pick up a bit of glue off the stick with the blade of an old craft knife and slide the blade between the two elements that need to be glued back together.

Assembly

To hold together two parts that need to be able to move, you can interlock them together or link them with thread.

• Interlocking with open slits

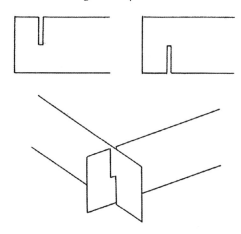

• Interlocking with a closed slit

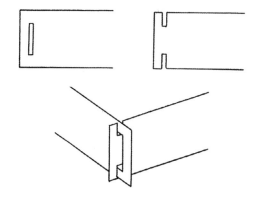

• Assembly with knotted or glued thread

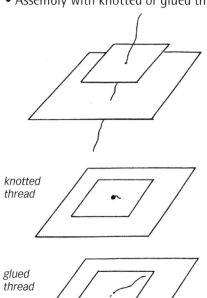

knotted thread

glued thread

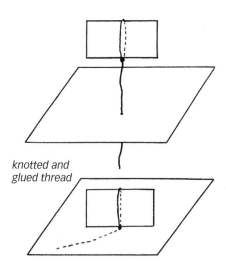

knotted and glued thread

O Christmas Tree

EASY

A Christmas tree all decorated to wish a loved one a very merry Christmas!

TOOLS

- Cutting Board
- Flat ruler
- Craft knife
- Glue stick
- Embossing stylus
- Scissors
- Hole punch

MATERIALS

- White A4 paper (160g)
- Forest green A4 paper (80g)
- Red, white, and yellow A4 papers (80g)

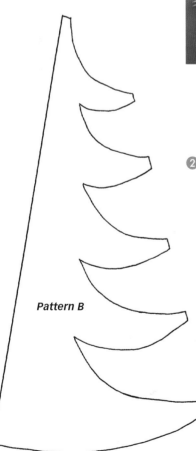

Pattern B

❶ Cutting and folding the tree

Attach pattern piece A (page 52) on top of one sheet of green paper. Cut away the part shaded with diagonal lines, then score all the fold lines. Make the mountain folds first, then the valley folds. Cut the outline of the Christmas tree (pattern piece B, below) from 80g white paper. Place this piece on the folded green paper, and trace the

outline with a pencil. Use scissors to cut away the excess, as shown on page 52.

❷ Decorating the tree

Glue little circles (or other shapes) cut from red and yellow paper with the hole punch onto the tree, or use little bits of colored adhesive. At the ends of the branches, glue two circles made from pattern piece C (below), to each side of the lower edge of the branch.

❸ Preparing the card

Cut the sheet of heavy white paper in half, score one half down the middle, fold it, and open it up again to get a double card 8³/₄ inches tall by 4 inches wide.

❹ Putting the tree and star in place

Fold the tree up again. Cover one side with glue and glue it along the bottom edge of the card, ¹/₁₆ inch from the central fold. Close up the card to help it stick, then open it. Spread glue on the other side of the tree, then close the card.

Cut the two parts of the star (D, below). Cover one half with glue and stick it to the card, on top of the tree, against the fold of the card. Glue the tail of the star inside the first fold of the tree. Proceed in the same way for the second half of the star, then glue several red and yellow circles onto the branches that are glued to the card.

Pattern D

Pattern C

12

Magic Lantern

Whether you make it in a simple or elaborate style, may this paper lantern guide you to the end of winter.

TOOLS

- Ruler
- Cutting board
- Craft knife
- Glue stick
- Embossing stylus
- Metal ruler

MATERIALS

- Beige or brown A5 cardstock (120g)
- Orange or red A5 cardstock (120g)

1 Preparing the lantern

Attatch the pattern below on the beige paper, cut it out, and score the fold lines. Take away the pattern and score again. Fold the three folds of the lantern in both directions. Fold the central fold in the opposite direction (valley) from the other two, and fold the tab on the left down (a mountain fold) and put glue on it.

2 Setting it up

Place the lantern in the scored A5 card. Keeping the valley fold of the lantern on the valley fold of the card, stick the tab on the left onto the card. Close the card, keeping the glued part steady. Open the card and fold the central fold of the lantern back into a mountain fold.

Put the two tops of the lantern together: fold the two legs of the left part and insert them into the slit in the part on the right, then unfold them again to keep the parts together.

Put the tab on the right flat and put glue on it. Fold the lantern again, and close the card. Press hard to help the glue stick well.

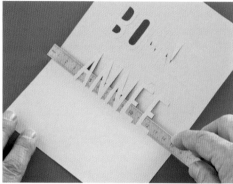

Happy New Year!

*W*rite it in many languages; may this new year be by far the best!

TOOLS

- Cutting board
- Flat ruler
- Pencil
- Craft knife
- Embossing stylus
- Small metal ruler

MATERIALS

- Tracing paper
- White or colored A5 paper (120 or 160g)

VARIATIONS

To write a single line of text, draw only one dashed line 4 inches from the lower edge of the tracing paper. To write three lines of text, draw three dashed lines (3 inches, 4³/₄ inches, and 6³/₄ inches from the edge) and two dotted lines (4¹/₄ inches and 6 inches from the edge).

❶ Preparing the tracing paper

Use a pencil to draw three horizontal lines on the tracing paper: two dashed lines and one dotted line, following diagram 1 below. Place the tracing paper on the pattern on page 53 and trace the letters, lining up the dashed lines on the tracing paper and the red dashed line on the pattern with each other. Don't forget to draw the dotted line on each letter.

After you've traced all the letters, erase the dashes on the insides of the letters, as well as the dots at the bottom of the top word.

❷ Making the card

Attach the tissue paper to the sheet of paper with paper clips, score the dotted and dashed lines, and cut out the letters. Take away the tissue paper and score the folds again (dashed and dotted lines).

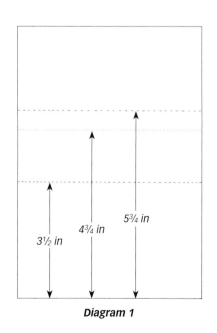

Diagram 1

3¹/₂ in
4³/₄ in
5³/₄ in

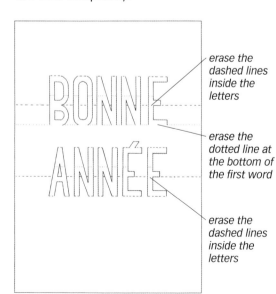

Slide the small ruler behind the letters at the base of the bottom word and use it to gently fold the letters. Slide the ruler to the top edge of the letters and make that fold in the same way. Place the ruler on its edge, under the interior fold of the letters. While holding the ruler in this position, make the fold by pinching the paper gently between your fingers. Also crease the fold created behind the letters.

Proceed in the same way with the other lines of text, and finish folding the card, pressing down on the folds to close the card completely.

erase the dashed lines inside the letters

erase the dotted line at the bottom of the first word

erase the dashed lines inside the letters

Diagram 2

С НОВЫМ ГОДОМ

FELIZ AÑO NUEVO

BONNE ANNÉE

HAPPY NEW YEAR

The new year is announced grandly on a pedestal.

TOOLS

- Cutting board
- Ruler
- Craft knife
- Embossing stylus
- Small metal ruler

MATERIALS

- A5 paper in the color of your choice (120 to 160g)

Making the card

Attach the pattern below to the center of the sheet of paper with paper clips, using the central fold as a reference point. Cut along the solid lines.

Score all the folds carefully.

Remove the pattern and score the folds again. Use the small ruler to help you pop up the card gradually, following the mountain and valley folds indicated on a pattern.

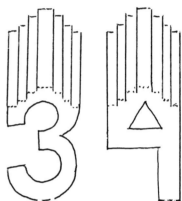

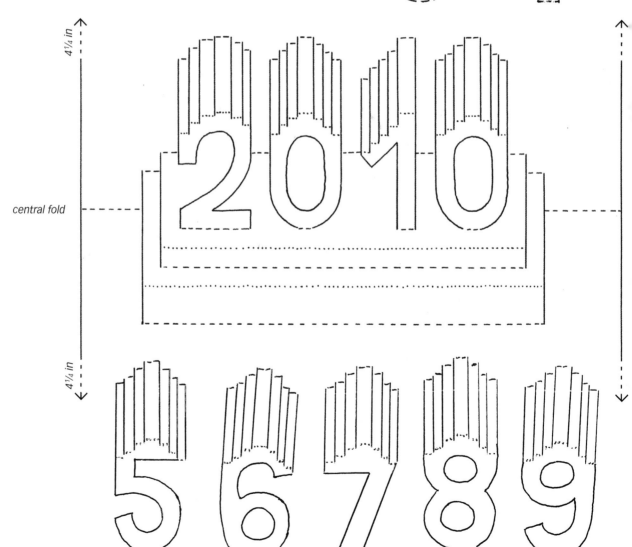

central fold

4¼ in

4¼ in

Snowman

EASY

F or making by the fireside to amuse the children— but not just the children!

TOOLS

- Cutting board
- Craft knife
- Glue stick
- Embossing stylus
- Paper clips

MATERIALS

- Folded and scored white A5 cardstock
- Light brown and ice blue A5 papers (160g)
- Red and dark brown A5 papers (120g)
- White A5 paper (80g)
- Blue and orange felt-tipped markers

① Preparing the snowman

Attach pattern piece A to the white paper, cut it out, and score the folds. Attach pattern piece B to the light brown paper and cut out the broom. Glue it onto the snowman at a slant. Attach pattern piece C to the red paper and cut it out. Glue the front and back of the scarf around the snowman's neck. Attach pattern piece D to the dark brown paper and cut out two of this hat. Glue them on either side of the head. Use markers to draw the eyes, mouth, and nose.

② Setting it up

Fold the tabs. Put glue on one of the tabs and stick it to the card, 1/16 inch from the main fold. Put glue on the second tab and close the card. Press hard along the edge of the card to help the glue stick. Open the card. Attach pattern piece E on the blue paper; cut out two of this shape. Put glue on these two half circles and stick them on the card to cover up the tabs.

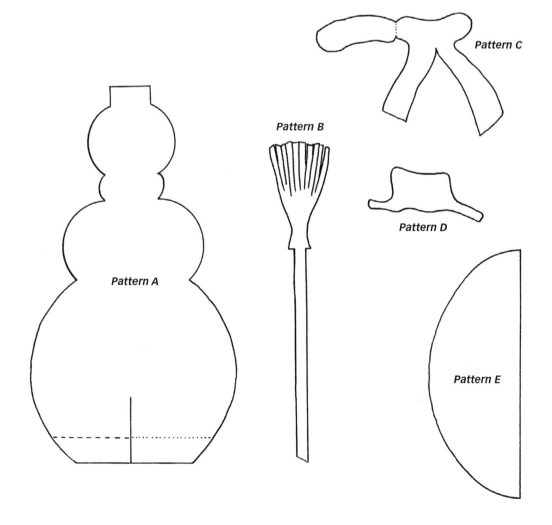

Pattern C

Pattern B

Pattern D

Pattern A

Pattern E

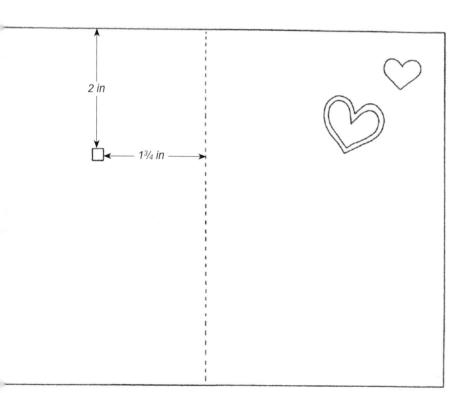

Be My Valentine

On February 14, give that special someone this card cut with love and brought to life by your magician's fingers.

TOOLS

- Cutting board
- Craft knife
- Glue stick
- Embossing stylus

MATERIALS

- White A5 paper (160g)
- Pink A5 paper (120g)

❶ Preparing the card

Attach pattern A (below) to the pink paper and cut out the hollow heart, starting by cutting on the inside. Put glue on the hollow heart and the little heart obtained in the process and glue them in the upper right-hand corner of the card. On the left part of the card, draw a square ¼ inch on each side, 2 inches from the top edge of the card and 1¾ inches from the central fold, as indicated in the diagram below.

❷ Attaching the heart

Attach pattern piece B (p 54) to the pink paper. Cut out the central heart and score all the fold lines. Remove the pattern, then score the fold lines again. Following the directions for the folds indicated on the pattern, fold the heart up on itself, including the tabs. Open the heart, put glue on the top of the left tab, and stick it to the card where you drew the box. Press hard to make sure the glue sticks.

Fold the heart up again. Put glue on the right tab and close the card. Press hard to help the glue adhere.

2 in

1¾ in

central fold

Pattern A

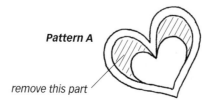

remove this part

It's Spring!

With his tulip, the harbinger of spring, this rabbit will delight little ones and grown-ups alike.

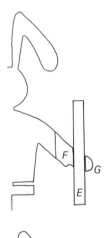

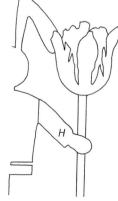

❶ Preparing the tulip

Photocopy the stem and leaf pattern (p 54), then cut the shapes out of green paper; score the fold line for the tab. Copy and cut out petal R and petal J (page 54): one of R in the red paper and two of J in the yellow paper. Put glue on the top ¼ inch of the stem and attach the red petal. Put glue on the bottom half of one of the yellow petals and stick it onto the red petal. Turn the second yellow petal over, put glue on the bottom half, and glue it under the red petal.

❷ Preparing the rabbit

Attach pattern pieces A and B (opposite page) on the tan paper and cut them out. Score the folds of the tabs. Cut out pattern C (opposite page) from white paper, then glue it to the body of the rabbit. Cut the two parts of the overalls out from red paper (pattern piece D, opposite page). Put glue on them and stick them to the body and leg of the rabbit.

❸ Assembling the rabbit and tulip

Photocopy and cut out pattern pieces E, F, G, and H (page 54): E from white paper and F, G, and H from tan paper. Turn the rabbit over. Put glue on the wrist, F, and place it on the rabbit's right arm. Put the strip of paper (E) in the rabbit's hand, right next to the wrist, but do not glue it (see the diagram, left). Put glue on the hand (G) and attach it next to the strip of paper on the rabbit's hand. Put glue on the top sides of F and G, take away the strip of paper, and put the stem of the tulip in its place, with the leaf turned to the outside. Put glue on the ½ inch of piece H closest to the shoulder, and stick it onto the right arm of the rabbit. Press down on the glue while moving the stem of the tulip up and down in the rabbit's hand.

❹ Gluing the rabbit and tulip to the grass

Photocopy the pattern for the grass (I, page 54) and cut it out from green paper; cut away the slots and score the fold. Remove the pattern and score the fold again. Fold the grass all the way in both directions, then open it flat. Insert the tab on the tulip into slot X and the tab on the rabbit's left foot into slot Y. Fold the grass in two. Fold and unfold the tabs, glue them, and fold them back onto the grass.

Turn the whole thing over and open the grass. Attach the rabbit's legs together by their slots, and insert the tab of the right foot into slot Z. Fold the grass in two again, fold and unfold the tab, glue it, and fold it back onto the grass.

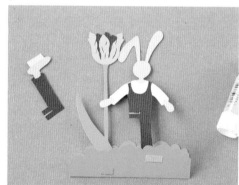

❺ Gluing the card

Cut a piece of A5 cardstock into two equal pieces. Put glue on one half of the grass and glue one half of the cardstock to it, ¹/₁₆ inch from the fold. Turn the whole thing around. Put glue on the other half of the grass and stick the other half of the cardstock to it, ¹/₁₆ inch from the fold.

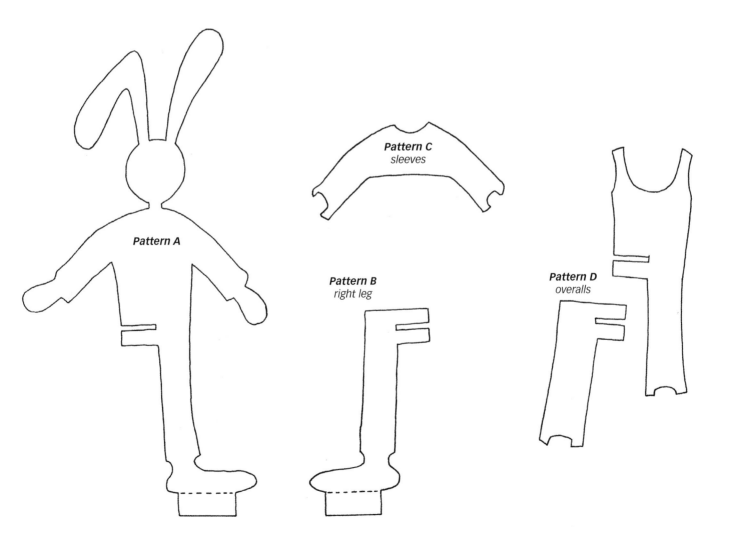

Pattern A

Pattern B
right leg

Pattern C
sleeves

Pattern D
overalls

An Easter Egg

DETAILED

Everyone into the garden! The bunny has already distributed multicolored eggs and delicious chocolates.

TOOLS

- Cutting board
- Flat ruler
- Craft knife
- Glue stick
- Embossing stylus
- Fine needle
- Small pliers/tweezers
- Scissors

MATERIALS

- White A5 cardstock
- White, ivory, and green A5 paper (160g)
- Red paper (120g)
- Beige thread

① Preparing the card

Cut out of green paper a square 4 inches on each side; score the diagonal. Mark two points on the other diagonal, $1/2$ inches on either side of the center. Prick holes at these two points with a needle, then fold the square completely in both directions. Cut an A5 piece of cardstock in two to get two rectangles $3/4$ by 4 inches.

② Making the egg

Photocopy the pattern below and the ones on page 55. Put piece A on red paper and the rest on ivory paper. Cut out the different part of the egg. Slide piece B through piece A and put their central slots together. Put the two C pieces on either side of piece B; put the central slots of the C pieces into the side slots on B. Add one D piece, putting the three lower slots through the lower slots of B and the two C pieces, then put the top slots of D together with the top slots of B and the two C pieces. Do the same with the other D piece.

③ Attaching the thread

Wrap a piece of beige thread around one of the D pieces at the level of a bottom side slot and make a double knot. Cut the shorter thread near the knot, thread the longer thread through a needle, and pass the needle through one of the holes in the green square. Keep the thread in place with a piece of tape. Take another length of thread and repeat this process with the other D piece, near the slot diametrically opposite the first, then put the threaded needle through the other hole in the green card.

④ Attaching the egg to the card

Take off the tape, pull on the threads under the square, and fold the square with the egg in the middle. Keeping the square closed, turn the egg 45 degrees.

Tighten the thread and put glue on half the square and the thread on that half, which must stay tight. Cut the part of the string that sticks out past the edge and stick on one half of the A5 card, $1/16$ inch from the fold in the square. Turn the whole thing over and do the same thing with the other half of the card.

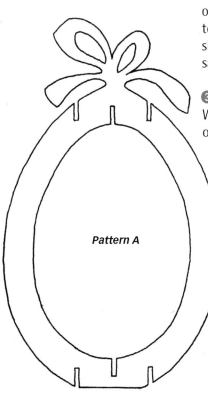

Pattern A

26

Happy Birthday!

No single gust of breath will extinguish the paper candles on this lovely birthday cake.

TOOLS

- Cutting board
- Craft knife
- Ruler
- Glue stick
- Embossing stylus
- Metal ruler
- Tweezers

MATERIALS

- White A5 cardstock (160g)
- Red, yellow, orange, and purple A5 papers (120g)

1 Preparing the card

Attach the pattern from page 56 to the A5 card with paper clips and cut it out. Carefully score all the folds. Take away the pattern and score all the folds again, firmly. Following the mountain and valley folds indicated on the pattern, pop the card up progressively. Use the tweezers for the folds on top of the cake. Fold the card completely.

2 Putting the candles in place

Cut fourteen candles out of the colored paper, using the patterns below. Cut out the heart of the flame first, and then cut out the outer edge.

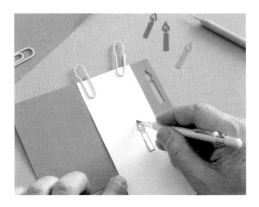

Open the card, put glue on the bottom ¼ inch of the candles, and attach the candles to the squares, just above the valley folds. Make sure they stick by pressing each candle onto its support with the tweezers.

VARIATION

You can replace the candles in the center of the cake with numbers with flames on top.

28

Pretty Yellow Butterfly

*O*pen it, close it—the butterfly poses, rests, or flies away
to another flower in turn.

TOOLS

- Cutting board
- Flat ruler
- Craft knife
- Glue stick
- Embossing stylus

MATERIALS

- White A5 cardstock (160g)
- Yellow, light blue, and dark blue A5 papers (120g)

❶ Preparing the card

Use a pencil to make a little cross on the cardstock, 1½ inches away from the top edge and ½ inch to the right of the central fold.

❷ Cutting out the butterfly

Attach the photocopy of the patten (pattern A on page 55) to a sheet of yellow paper with paper clips and cut out the wings of the butterfly. Start with the interior cuts and finish with the outside edge. Score the folds of the two tabs.

❸ Attaching the right wing

Fold the tab back on the right wing and put glue on it, without going over the edges. Position the wing on the card: the body of the butterfly against the central fold, the end of the antenna just under the cross you marked. Holding the wing in this position, fold the tab back to attach it to the card. Close the card, pressing lightly on the glued part.

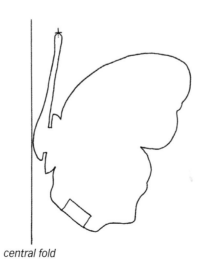

central fold

❹ Attaching the left wing

Open the card. Put the two wings together by passing the antenna of the right wing through the slot in the left wing. Then place the left wing on the right wing. Put glue on the tab without going over the edges. Close the card and press lightly to fix the second wing well in place.

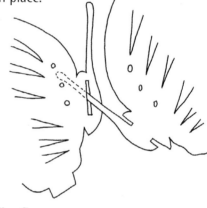

❺ The flower

Photocopy the petals (B) and sepals (C), from page 55. Cut out the six petals in light blue paper and the six sepals in dark blue paper. Glue the sepals on top of the petals. Glue the two split petals onto the card, sliding them around the bases of the butterfly's wings. Glue the other four petals onto the card. Make sure none of the petals cover the central fold.

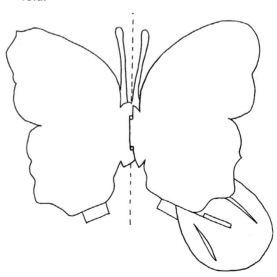

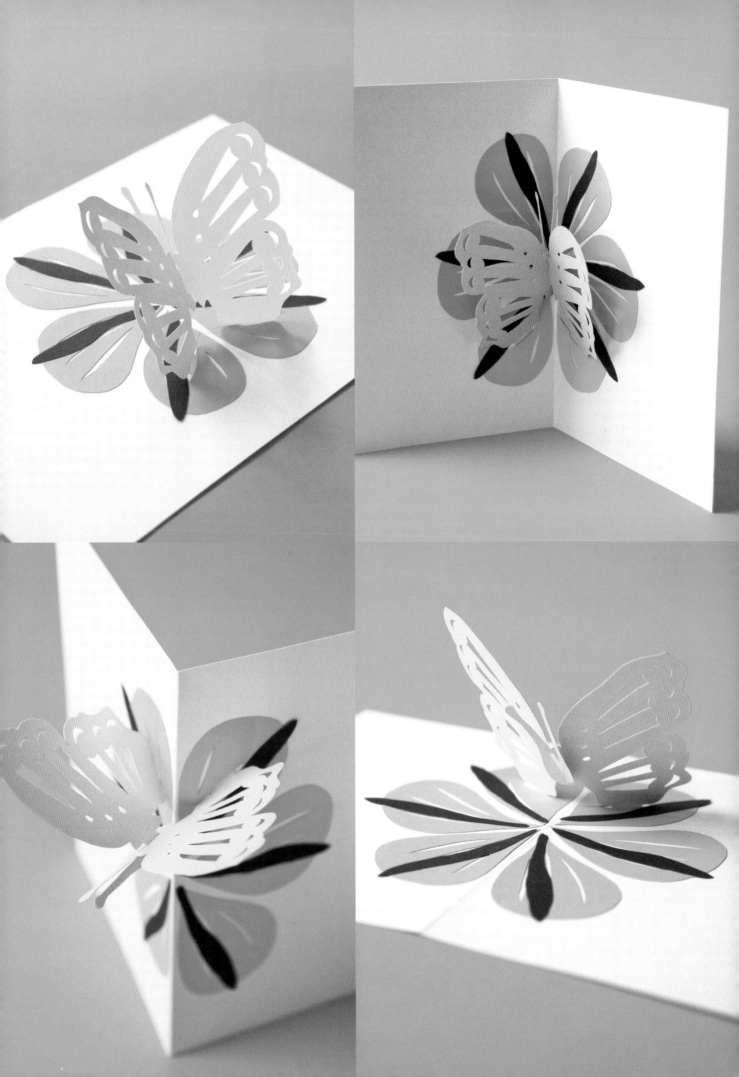

Honeycomb

DETAILED

Create a honeycomb, playing endlessly with the shapes and colors.

TOOLS

- Cutting board
- Ruler
- Craft knife
- Glue stick
- Embossing stylus
- Metal ruler
- Scissors

MATERIALS

- Beige and orange A5 papers (160g)

❶ Preparing the card

Attach the pattern over the center of the beige paper with paper clips, using the central fold as a reference point; cut it out. Carefully score all the fold lines. Remove the pattern and score the fold lines again firmly. With the help of a ruler and carefully following the mountain and valley folds indicated on the pattern, progressively pop the card up.

Close the card completely and flatten it out. Open the card and bring it back completely to a flat sheet. Use the craft knife to cut out the insides of the hexagons, leaving an edge of ¹⁄₈ inch around each hexagon. Fold the card up again. Get rid of the central fold by cutting ¹⁄₁₆ inch away with scissors from each side.

❷ The colored background

Score the orange paper and fold it in two. Put glue on one half of the honeycomb and glue it onto the orange paper, overlapping the edges. Put glue on the other half of the honeycomb, then close the card and press to help the glue stick.

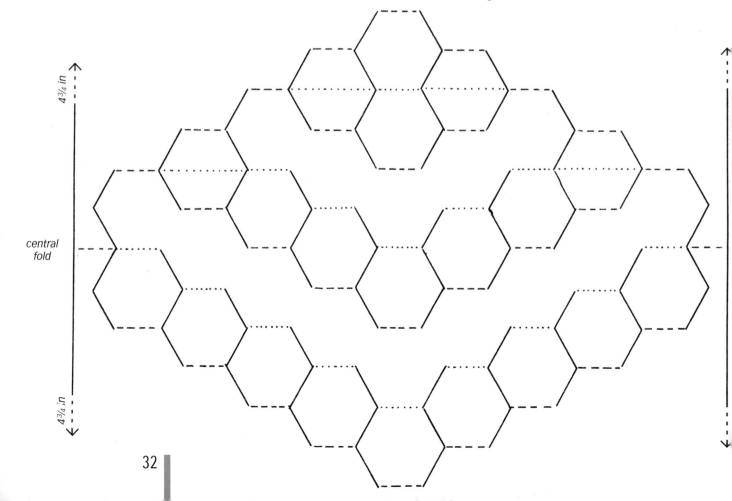

4³⁄₄ in

central fold

4³⁄₄ in

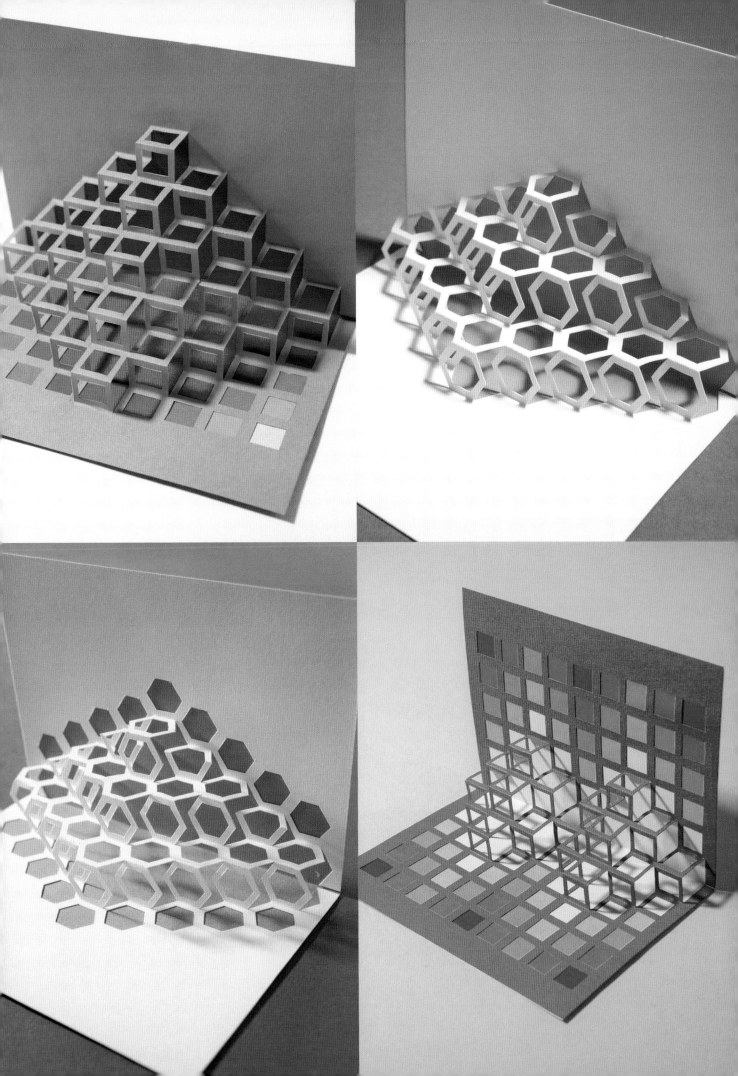

Bluets

DETAILED

"Say it with flowers"—it's always a pleasure. These lovely bluets will say it longer than real ones!

TOOLS

- Cutting board
- Craft knife
- Glue stick
- Emobssing stylus
- Small ruler

MATERIALS

- Beige A4 paper (160g)
- Green and light blue A5 papers (160g)

❶ Preparing the card

Cut the beige sheet of paper in two lengthwise. Attach the pattern from page 57 to one half of the sheet (11³/₄ by 4 inches) with paper clips. Cut it out, then score all the fold lines. Remove the pattern and score the fold lines again. Use the small ruler to pop the card up, following the directions of the folds indicated on the pattern.

❷ Attaching the stems

Attach pattern A (below) to the green paper and cut out the three groups of stems and leaves. Put glue on them, except for the parts shaded in gray below, then stick them to the card.

❸ Gluing the flowers

Attach pattern B (below) to the blue paper and cut out the two flowers. Put glue on the parts shaded in gray below, then glue the flowers onto the card. Fold the card up and make sure the glue sticks by pressing hard.

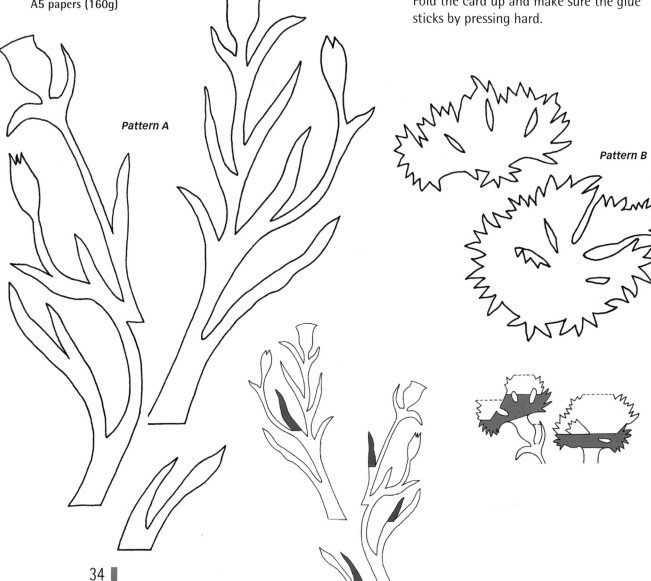

Pattern A

Pattern B

Love
Rosie

A Day at the Beach

Lounge chair, umbrella, and the ocean as far as the eye can see . . . an invitation to complete idleness.

TOOLS

- Cutting board
- Craft knife
- Glue stick
- Embossing stylus
- Small ruler

MATERIALS

- Beige A4 paper (160g)
- Blue, purple, brown, yellow, and red A5 papers (80g)

Pattern B

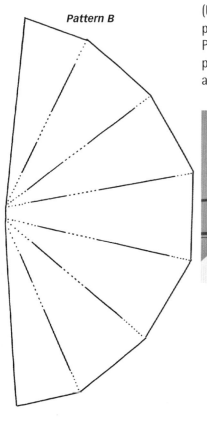

1 Preparing the card

Cut the beige sheet of paper in half lengthwise. Attach the pattern from page 58 to a half sheet of the beige paper (11³/₄ by 4 inches) with paper clips. Cut carefully, then score the fold lines. Remove the pattern and score the fold lines again. Use a pencil to draw a square ³/₈ inch on each side in the extension of the umbrella pole and ¹/₂ inch above the pole, as indicated in diagram 1 on page 58.

Pop up the card, following the directions of the folds indicated on the pattern. Fold the top left part of the deck chair, insert the top right part, then the left part in the slot just above the deck chair. Fold the refolded left part to the back of the card. Attach pattern A (below) to the second piece of beige paper and cut out the umbrella ribs. Put glue onto the horizontal part of the pole of the umbrella on the card and attach the ribs to it.

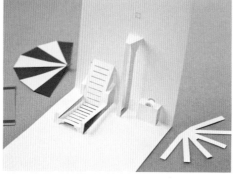

2 Assembling the umbrella

Attach pattern piece B (below) to the red paper, cut it out, and score the fold lines. Remove the pattern, score again, fold it, then unfold it. Attach pattern C (below) to the yellow paper and cut out the three triangles; apply glue to them and attach them to the red paper, alternating the colors. Attach pattern D from page 58 to the brown paper, cut it out, and score. Put glue on the part indicated and stick it to the top, in the center and back of the red paper, making it stick out past the rounded part. Put glue on the rounded portion of the umbrella and glue it onto the square drawn on the card.

3 The beach towel

Attach pattern piece E (page 58) to the blue paper and cut it out. Attach pattern piece F (page 58) to the purple paper, cut out two stripes, and glue them on the ends of the blue towel. Put glue on the towel and stick it to the card, to the side of the deck chair.

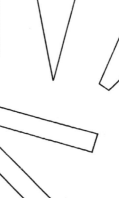

Pattern A

Pattern C

A Day on the Water

*F*or a solitary adventure or a little cruise, train with this sailboat!

TOOLS

- Cutting board
- Craft knife
- Glue stick
- Embossing stylus
- Paper clips
- Ruler

MATERIALS

- Light blue A5 cardstock (160g)
- Orange, brown, and dark blue A5 papers (120g)
- White A5 paper (80g)

❶ Preparing the card

Score the cardstock and fold it completely in half (widthwise) in both directions. open the card and use a pencil to draw a square $3/8$ inch on each side, $2\frac{1}{2}$ inches from the edge of the card and $3/8$ inch from the fold, as shown in the diagram on page 59.

❷ Setting up the sails and the mast

Attach pattern piece A (below) to the brown paper and pattern piece B (page 59) to the white paper. Cut the piece out and glue the three corners of sail B to mast A. Attach pattern C to the white paper, cut out, and glue this sail to the front of the mast. Attach pattern piece D to the brown paper and pattern piece E to the orange paper; cut out the pieces and glue sail E and mast D.

Put a bit of glue at the top of mast A and at the front of the horizontal part of the mast and stick mast D to it, lining up the masts with each other. Fold back the tabs at the bottoms of the masts and put glue on them. Stick the tab of mast D on the square you marked on the card, and close the card. Hold it in place a few moments so the glue has a chance to set up.

❸ Popping up the boat

Attach patterns F and G (page 59) to the dark blue paper, cut them out, and score the fold lines. Put the two sides of the boat together. Fold one of the tabs back so you can insert both tabs through the slot, then unfold the folded tab. Open the card. Put the assembled boat flat, then fold back and put glue on the undersides of the two bases. Place the boat on both sides of the masts.

Unfold one of the bases and stick it to the card, $1/16$ inch from the central fold, putting the slot in the base around the base of the mast. Do the same with the second base.

Put glue on about the back $1/2$ inch of one of the sides of the boat and stick it to the other side of the boat. Press it in between your thumb and index finger and hold it for several seconds.

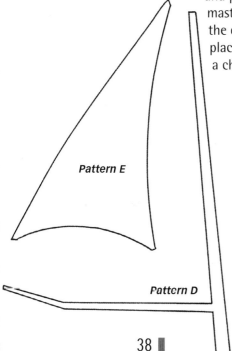

Pattern E

Pattern D

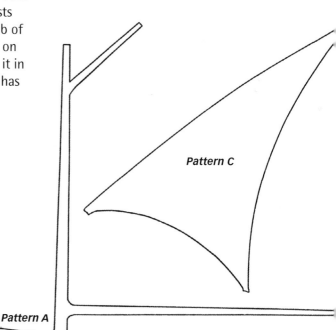

Pattern C

Pattern A

Seagulls

*D*aydream while watching this graceful ballet of seagulls,
but don't leave your picnic unattended!

TOOLS

- Ruler
- Cutting board
- Craft knife
- Glue stick
- Embossing stylus
- Small tweezers

MATERIALS

- Sky blue A5 cardstock (160g)
- White A5 paper (160g)
- Dark blue, medium blue, emerald green, and white A5 papers (80 to 120g)
- Yellow marker

❶ Preparing the card

Score the cardstock and fold in half. Use a pencil to draw a rectangle ½ by ¼ inch in the top left corner, as shown in the diagram below.

❷ The sea

Attach the patterns from page 60 on the papers: A on the dark blue paper, B and D on the white paper (80 g), C on the medium blue paper, and E on the green paper. Cut out the shapes and glue the papers on top of each other (top to bottom: green, white, medium blue, white, and dark blue). Cut the ocean obtained into two equal parts, 4 inches long each. Glue these strips on the bottom of the card, ¹/₁₆ inch from the central fold on each side. Attach the pattern below to the white paper (80g) and cut out the four little seagulls. Glue them to the left side of the card above the sea.

❸ The seagull

Attach the pattern below to the heavier white paper and cut out the large seagull. Score the fold lines, remove the pattern, and score again. Put a little bit of yellow (marker or paint) on the beak.

Put glue on the tab on the right wing and stick it to the rectangle marked of the card. Close the card and hold it closed several seconds.

Open the card and fold the seagull back on itself. Fold the tab on the left wing and apply glue to it generously. Keeping the seagull and the tab folded, close the card. Hold it in place for several seconds. Open the card gently and press on the tabs under the wings to make sure these spots are glued firmly, as they will be put to the test when the card is opened to 90 degrees.

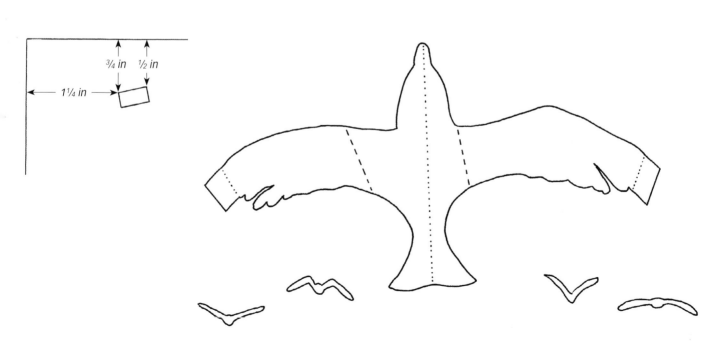

A New Baby!

VERY EASY

Hearts fly up to announce a birth, or congratulate the happy parents.

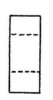

❶ Cutting out the card

Use paper clips to attach the pattern from page 56 to a sheet of unscored white paper, using the central fold as a reference point. Cut the pattern out, then score all the fold lines firmly. Remove the pattern and make sure that all the cut parts come apart (make sure especially that the angles are cut well). Then score all the folds lines again.

❷ The wheels

Cut two circles about ¼ inch in diameter from pink paper with an office hole punch. Glue these two circles in the centers of the wheels on the card.

❸ Popping up the baby buggy

Mark the mountain and valley folds on the pattern. Use the small ruler and your fingers to progressively form all the folds on the card. Fold gently, then go back over each fold to reinforce it. The buggy is fully popped up when the two sides of the card form a 90-degree angle. Fold the card completely, as if to put it in an envelope, then open it completely to flatten it out again.

❹ The hearts

Attach the pattern at left to the pink paper and cut out the hearts and their support. Remove the pattern and turn the hearts over. On the back of the largest heart, use a pencil to make a line parallel to the edge of the cropped bottom heart, 1½ inches above that edge (see diagram 1).

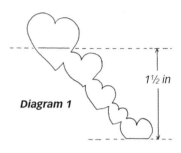

Diagram 1

1½ in

Score the fold lines on the tabs of the support. Fold them back and put glue on one of the two tabs. Stick it to the heart, just under the marked line (see diagram 2). Bend back the second tab and turn the hearts back over.

Diagram 2

❺ Attaching the hearts

Put glue on the tab in the middle of the buggy and stick the cropped heart to this tab, sliding it a little under the hood of the buggy. Press firmly to ensure it adheres. Gently lift up the largest heart. Put glue on the second tab of the support, without going over the edge, then close the card. Press to make sure the glue adheres.

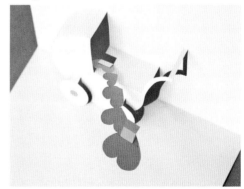

A Birthday Party

A pretty banner of paper letters, carried by two elephants, a giraffe for a guest—let the party begin!

TOOLS

- Cutting board
- Flat ruler
- Craft knife
- Glue stick
- Embossing stylus
- Paper clips
- Small ruler

MATERIALS

- White A5 paper (160g)
- Gray, red, and yellow A5 papers (120g)

❶ Preparing the card

Attach the pattern from page 61 to a piece of white paper. Cut out the pattern, then score the fold lines. Remove the pattern and score all the folds again. Following the directions of the folds indicated on the pattern, pop up the card with the small ruler. Fold it completely.

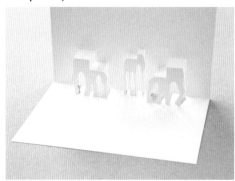

❷ Cutting out the animals and the banner

Cut out the shapes below: the giraffe from yellow paper, the elephant twice from gray paper, and the banner with the text from red paper.

❸ Gluing the animals

Open the card to 90 degrees. Put glue on the legs and body of the giraffe on the card, then stick the yellow giraffe onto the card, placing the bottoms of the feet $^{1}/_{16}$ inch above the fold.

Put glue on the legs and bodies of the elephants on the card, then stick the two gray elephants on, with their heads toward the outside, placing the bottoms of the feet $^{1}/_{16}$ inch above the fold. Close the card and press to ensure that the glue adheres.

❹ Gluing the text

Put glue on the leftmost $^{1}/_{2}$ inch of the banner with the text. Stick this end behind the trunk of the elephant on the left, letting $^{1}/_{4}$ inch stick over the edge, then bend the excess around the trunk of the elephant. Put glue on the rightmost end of the banner, from $^{1}/_{2}$ inch from the end to $^{1}/_{4}$ inch from the end. Stick it behind the trunk of the second elephant, letting the end stick out by $^{1}/_{2}$ inch. Bend the end back around the tunk of the elephant.

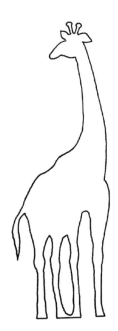

Snail

Where is he? At the edge of a fallen leaf, because autumn is here, and the snail is very happy!

TOOLS

- Cutting board
- Flat ruler
- Craft knife
- Glue stick
- Embossing stylus
- Fine needle
- Little tweezers
- Scissors

MATERIALS

- Green A4 paper (160g)
- White, cream, and brown A5 papers (160g)
- Yellow A5 paper (120g)
- Brown thread

❶ Preparing the card

Attach the pattern of the leaf (page 62) on the green paper, pierce points X and Y with the needle, and firmly crease the vertical fold. Cut around the outline of the leaf, remove the pattern, score the leaf, and fold it several times in both directions.

❷ Making the snail

Cut out the different parts of the snail: piece A (opposite page) in cream-colored paper, and the others (on the opposite page and on page 62) in brown paper. Slide piece B through A and interlock the central slots. Put the head of the snail through ring C and put the central slots of the ring through the forward slots on A. Put the tail of the snail through ring D and put the central slots of the ring through the rear slots of A. Put rings B, C, and D through ring E on one side; interlock first the three lower slots of right E with the slots in B, C, and D, then interlock the top slots. Do the same with ring F on the other side.

❸ Attaching the threads

With a needle threaded with brown thread (about 10 inches), make a double knot around ring C in the front left slot. Slide the knot toward the bottom. Pass the needle through hole X in the leaf, and hold the thread in place under the leaf with a bit of tape.

Remove the needle from the first thread and thread it with a second length of thread, and repeat the same process with ring D and the back right slot on the snail. Pass the needle through hole Y in the leaf.

❹ Attaching the snail to the card

Cut the white paper in half to obtain two pieces about 14 7/8 by 4 inches. Fold the leaf with the snail in the middle. Detach the tape, pull on the threads, and attach them to the back of the leaf with two new pieces of tape. Cut the threads where the stick out past the edge of the leaf. Put glue on one half of the leaf, paying close attention to the thread, which must be well glued. Stick one of the rectangles of white paper to the leaf, 1/16 inch from the fold line. Press firmly on the glued area. Put glue on the other half of the leaf and attach the second white rectangle, 1/16 inch from the fold line.

❺ The butterfly

Cut out the two wings below. Score and fold the tabs. Put glue on the tab of the right wing and stick it to the leaf, with the body of the butterfly parallel to the fold in the leaf, 1/8 inch away from the fold line. Assemble the two wings by interlocking the slots. Put glue on the tab on the left wing, then close the card.

Left wing   Right wing

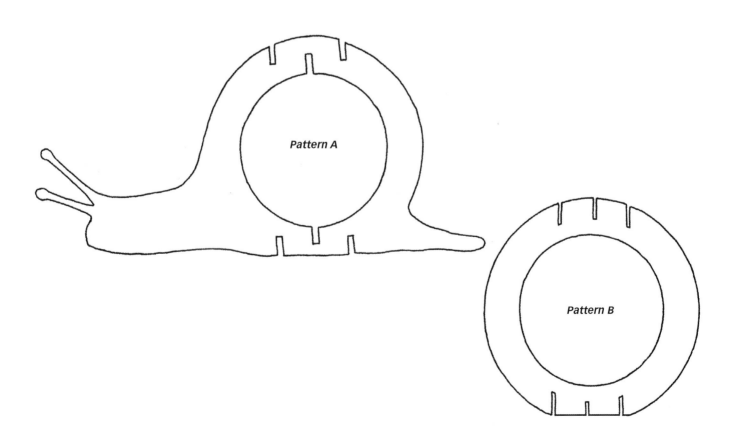

Pattern A

Pattern B

Windmill

EASY

All it needs is a breath, a light breeze, or just a bit of imagination.

TOOLS

- Cutting board
- Craft knife
- Ruler
- Embossing stylus
- Fine needle
- Scissors
- Small ruler

MATERIALS

- Ivory (160g) and brown (120 or 160g) A4 papers
- Brown thread

❶ Preparing the card

Attach the pattern from page 63 to the ivory paper, cut it out, score the fold lines, and pierce the center of the little cross with the needle. Remove the pattern and score again. Following the directions of the fold lines indicated on the pattern, use the small ruler to pop up the card.

❷ Cutting out the blades

Attach the pattern below to the brown paper and cut it out carefully, starting with the insides of the sails. Pierce the central point with the needle. Do the same thing with the circle.

❸ Attaching the wings

Cut about 10 inches of thread and thread it through the needle; position the needle in the middle of the thread and knot the two ends together. Pass the needle through the back of the windmill, through the hole you made earlier, and string on the brown circle, and then the wings, through the central hole. Make a knot and cut the excess thread.

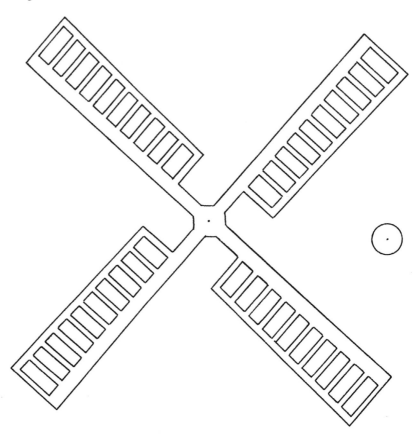

The Eternal Eiffel Tower

VERY EASY

People come to see it from all over the world . . . what would Paris be without your tower, Monsieur Eiffel?

TOOLS

- Cutting board
- Flat ruler
- Craft knife
- Glue stick
- Embossing stylus

MATERIALS

- Gray A4 paper (160g)
- Light brown A5 paper (160 or 210g)
- Green A5 paper (80g)

❶ Preparing the card

Cut the sheet of gray paper in half lengthwise. Score the fold in the middle, fold the card completely in both directions, then open it. On one of the halves, mark the placement of two of the feet of the tower by drawing two rectangles $1/10$ by $4/10$ inch, $3/4$ inch from the fold and 1 inch from the edges of the card, with a pencil. Use the diagram below.

Cut pattern piece A out of the green paper four times; these represent the garden plots surrounding the tower. Put glue on them and stick them to the card, $3/4$ inch from the fold, following the diagram below.

❷ Setting up the tower

Cut out the Eiffel tower (pattern on page 64) from the brown paper. Score the fold lines, remove the pattern, and score them again.

Cut a second tower shape and score the fold lines in the same way. Put glue on the top 1 inch of the two copies and stick them to each other, lining them up carefully. Fold the bases of the feet back. Put glue on the two bases of one copy of the tower and stick them to the card on the places you marked earlier. Press to ensure the glue adheres. Put glue on the bases of the second copy of the tower and close the card. Press down on the areas where the glue is.

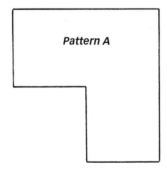

Pattern A

central fold

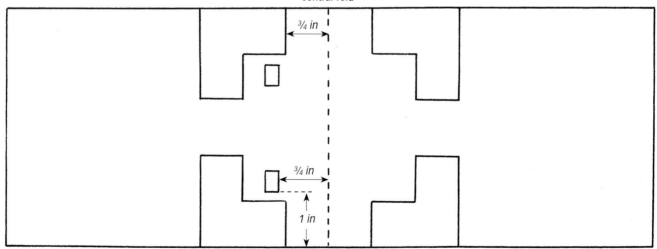

3/4 in

3/4 in

1 in

Patterns

Folding and cutting out "O Christmas Tree," page 12

Pattern A

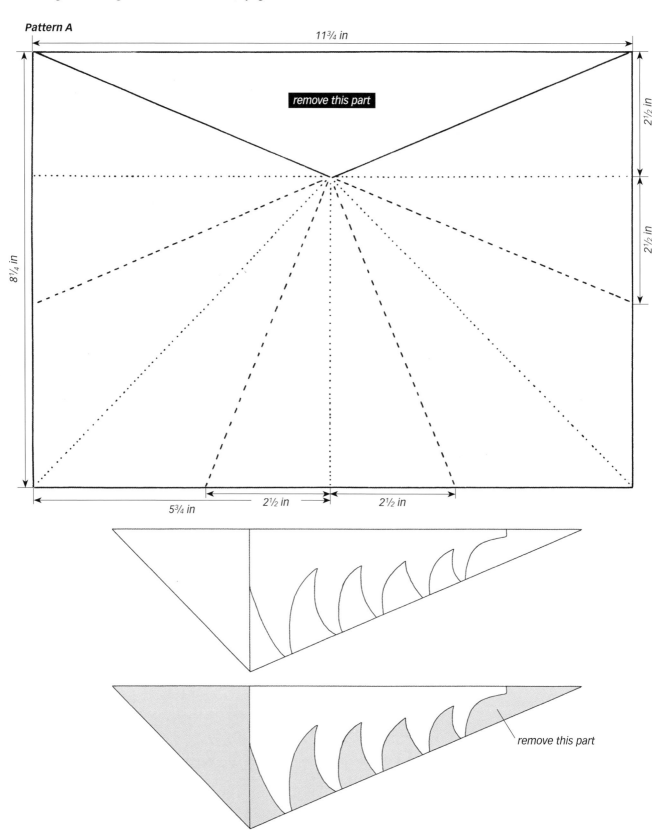

11¾ in

remove this part

2½ in

2½ in

8¼ in

5¾ in

2½ in

2½ in

remove this part

Patterns

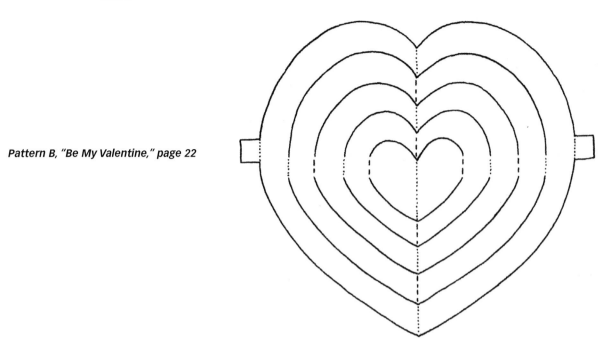

Pattern B, "Be My Valentine," page 22

Patterns for "It's Springtime!" page 24

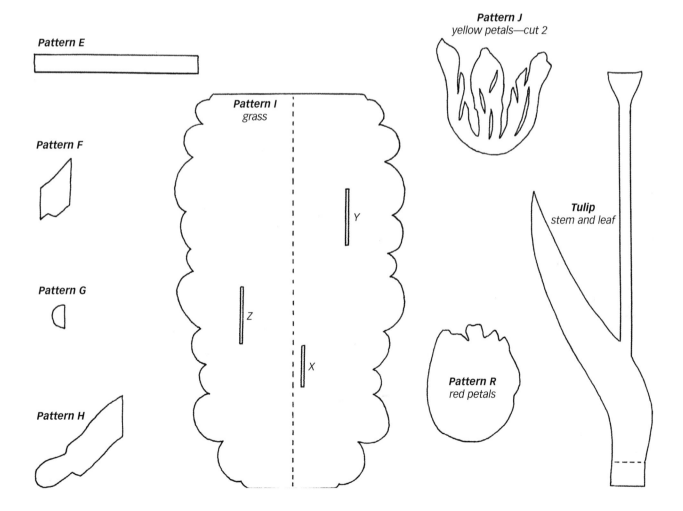

Pattern E

Pattern F

Pattern G

Pattern H

Pattern I
grass

Y

Z

X

Pattern J
yellow petals—cut 2

Tulip
stem and leaf

Pattern R
red petals

Patterns for "An Easter Egg," page 26

Patterns for "Pretty Yellow Butterfly," page 30

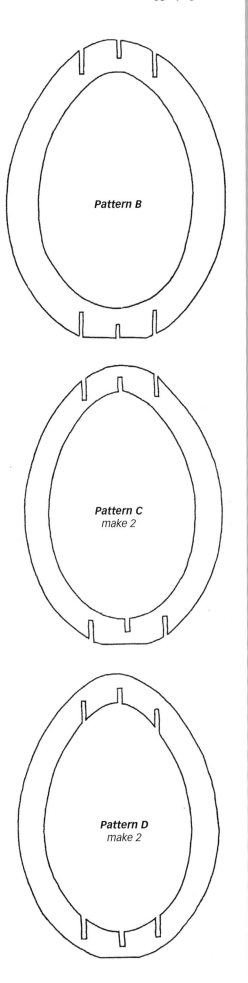

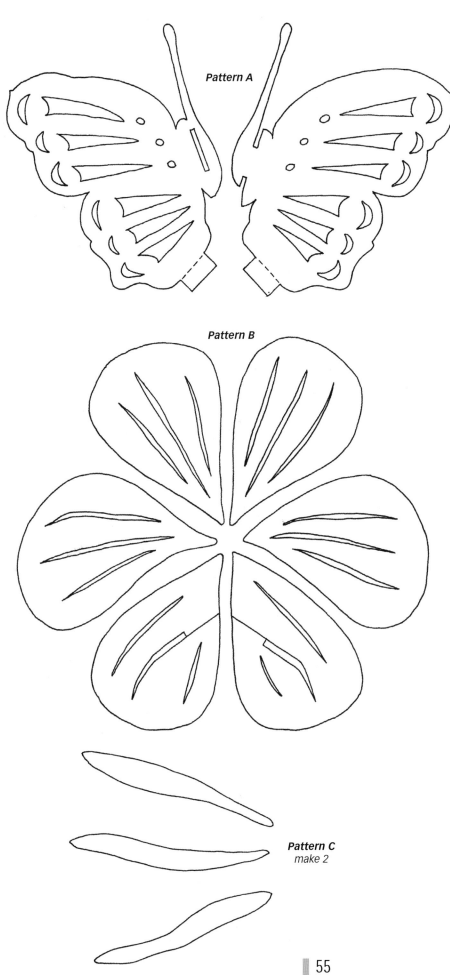

 Patterns

Pattern for "Happy Birthday," page 28

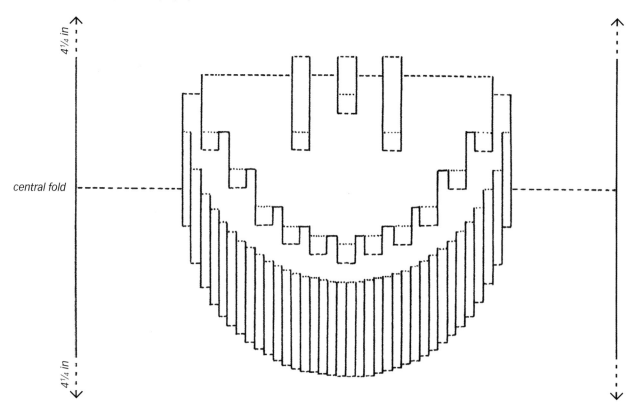

4¼ in

central fold

4¼ in

Pattern for "A New Baby !" page 42

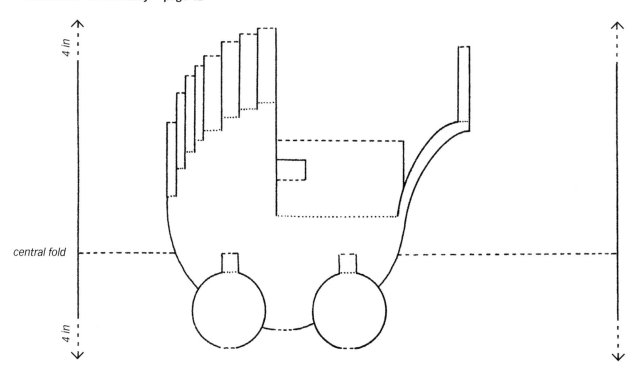

4 in

central fold

4 in

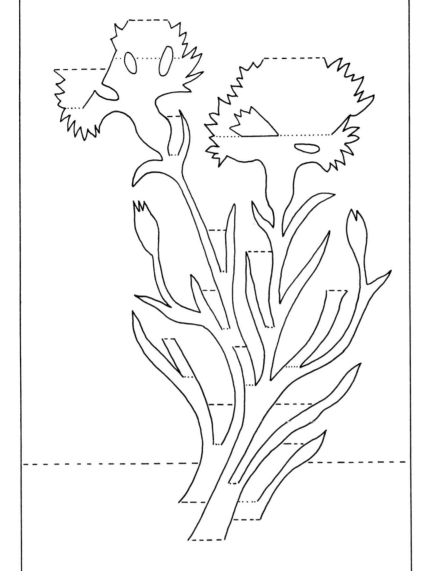

central fold

Patterns

**Patterns and diagram for
"A Day at the Beach," page 36**

Diagram 1

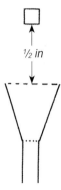

½ in

Pattern D

central fold

glue this part

Pattern F

Pattern E

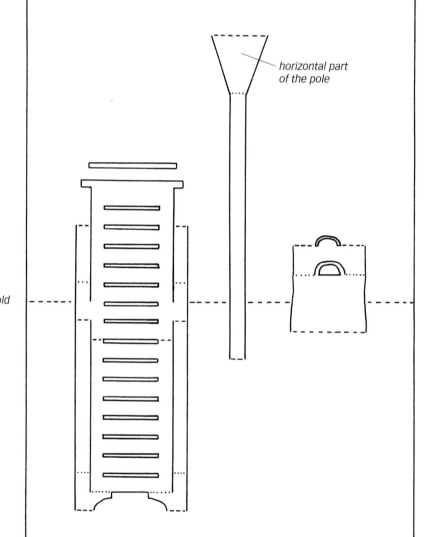

horizontal part
of the pole

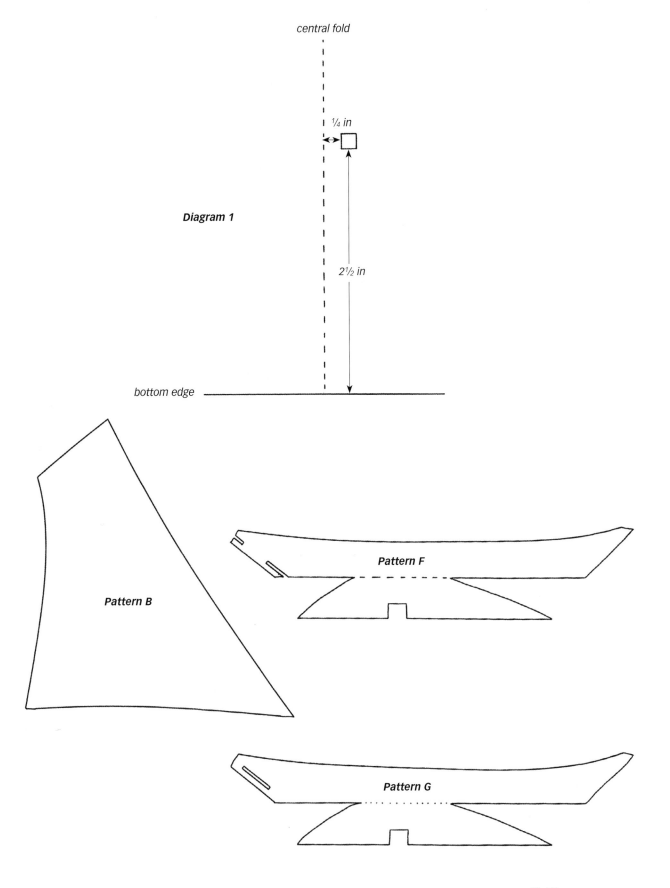

central fold

¼ in

2½ in

Diagram 1

bottom edge

Pattern B

Pattern F

Pattern G

Patterns

Patterns for the sea, "Seagulls," page 40

Pattern A

Pattern B

Pattern C

Pattern D

Pattern E

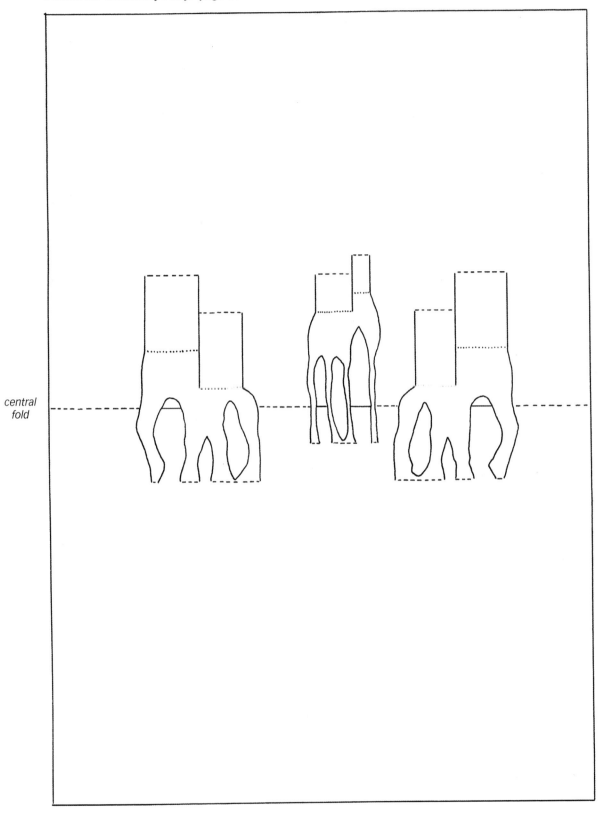

central
fold

 Patterns

Patterns for "Snail," page 46

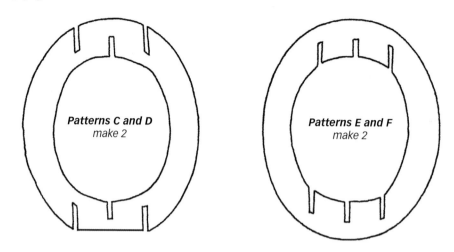

Patterns C and D
make 2

Patterns E and F
make 2

Pattern for the leaf

central fold

X · · Y

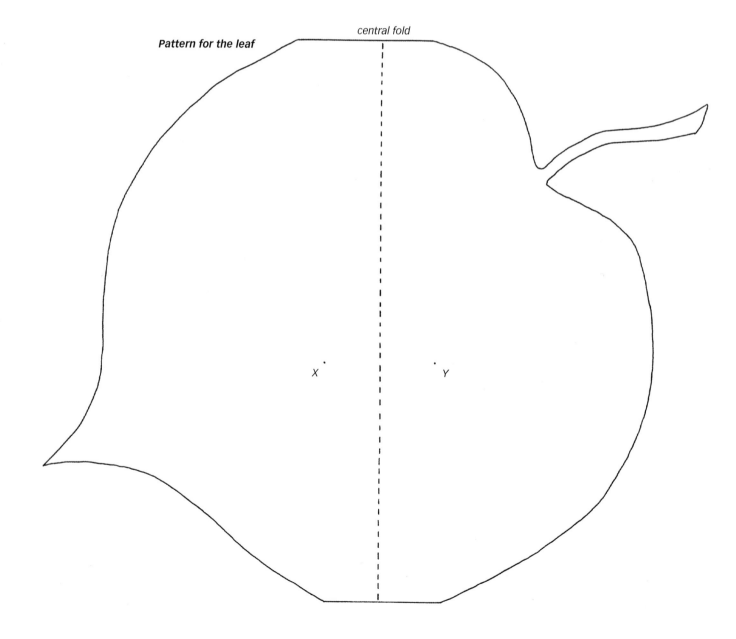

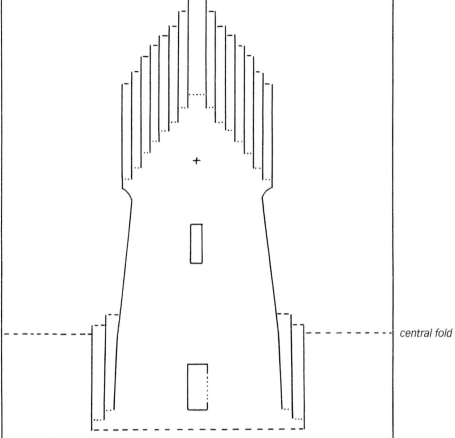

central fold

 Patterns

Pattern for "The Eternal Eiffel Tower," page 50

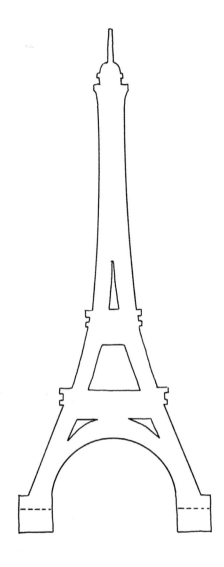

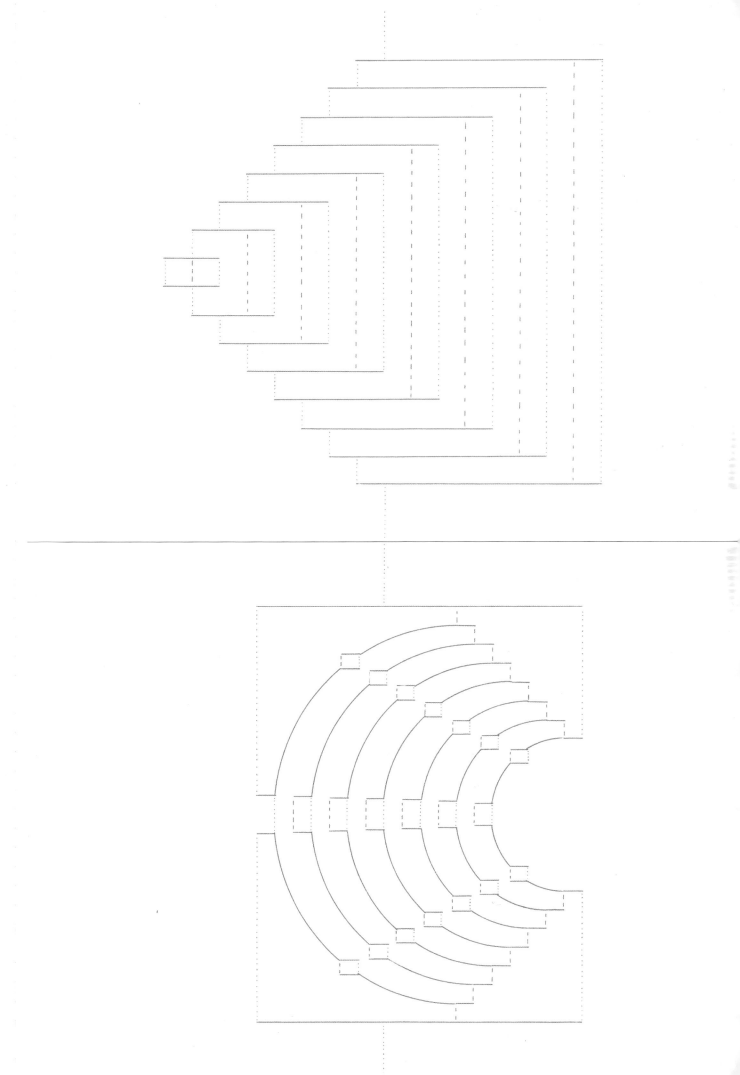

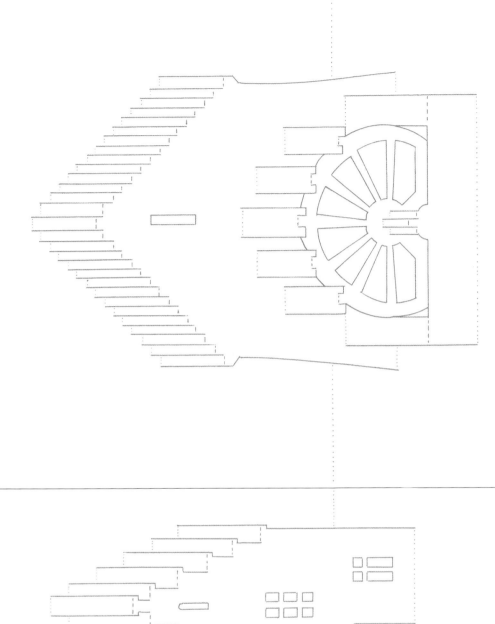
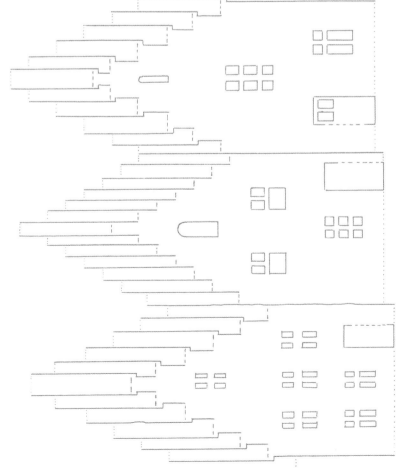

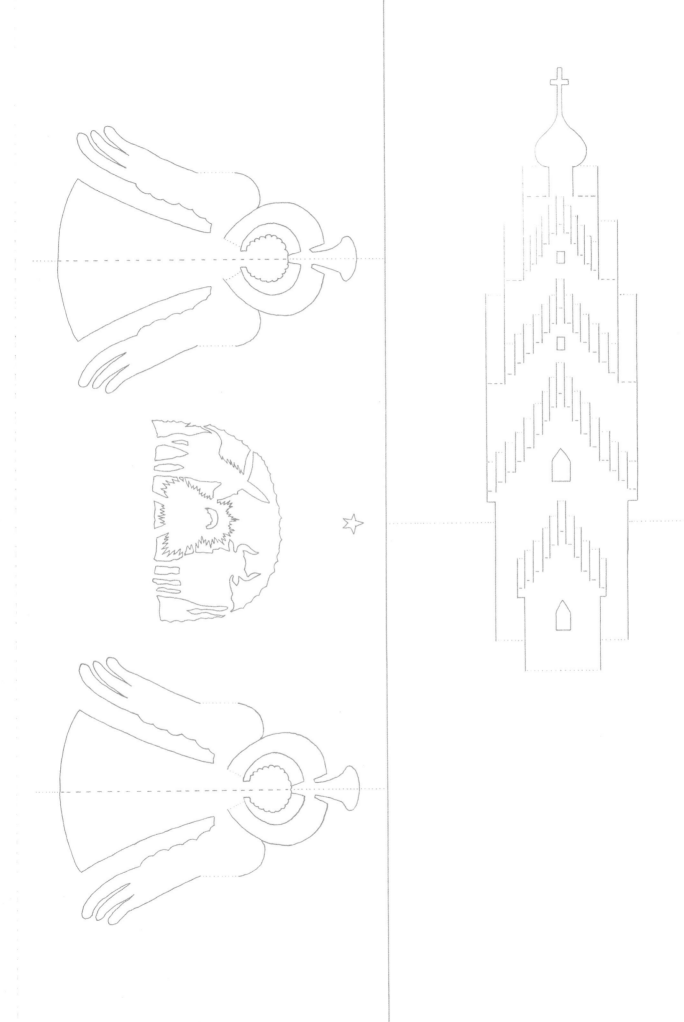

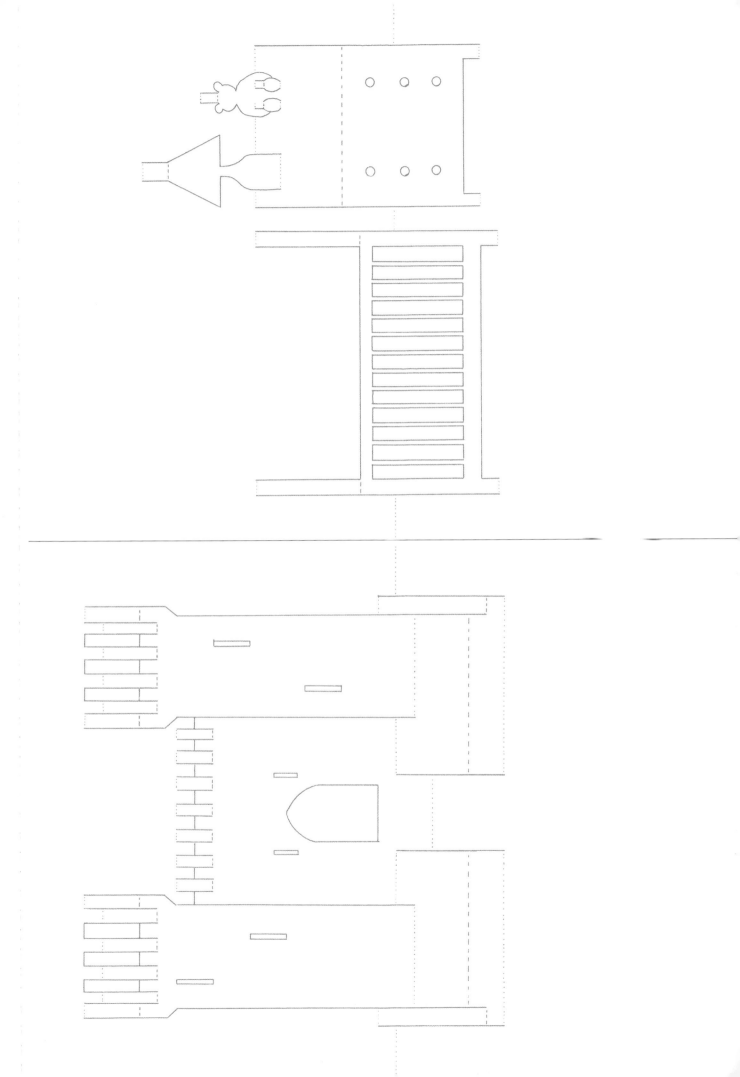

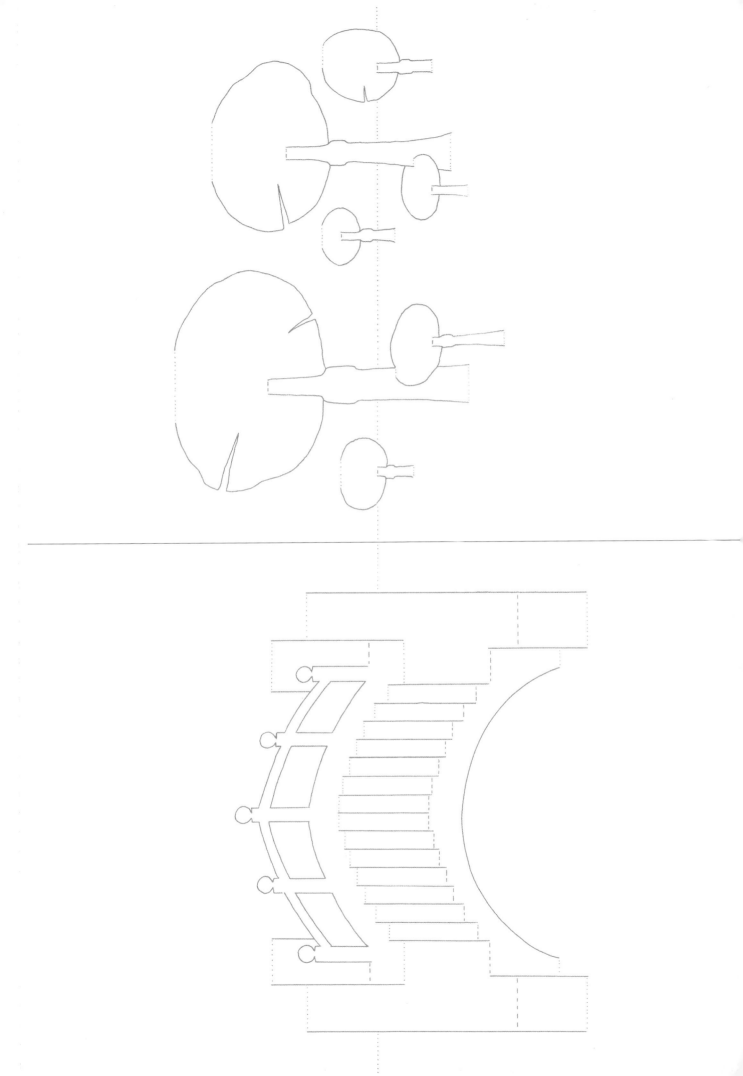